Original title:
Lessons in Loss

Copyright © 2024 Swan Charm
All rights reserved.

Author: Eliora Lumiste
ISBN HARDBACK: 978-9916-79-045-8
ISBN PAPERBACK: 978-9916-79-046-5
ISBN EBOOK: 978-9916-79-047-2

The Quiet Strength of Remembering

In whispers soft, the past can speak,
Echoes linger, memories seek.
Time holds still, yet gently flows,
In silent hearts, the knowing grows.

Faces fade but love remains,
Through joy and heartache, life sustains.
Each moment cherished, a gentle thread,
We weave the stories of those who've fled.

In twilight's glow, we sit and ponder,
The lessons learned, the dreams that wander.
With every thought, a hope ignites,
The quiet strength in starry nights.

With every breath, we hold them near,
In laughter's dance, in fallen tear.
A bridge of time, we reach across,
Their spirit lives, in love, not loss.

Through seasons' shift, our hearts entwine,
In sacred bonds, their light will shine.
The quiet strength in remembering
Fosters peace, a song we sing.

Whispers in the Void

In shadows deep where silence dwells,
Echoes dance like distant bells.
A breath of night, a glimmer faint,
Secrets held that words can't paint.

Stars above in velvet skies,
Whisper truths that never die.
With every sigh, a story flows,
In stillness, endless beauty grows.

The void remembers all it hears,
Carrying hopes, dreams, and fears.
A gentle touch, the absence sings,
In quiet realms, the heart takes wings.

When Silence Speaks

When silence speaks, the world stands still,
In hushed moments, we feel its thrill.
A gentle pause, a breath so deep,
In echoes lost, the memories keep.

In twilight's glow, the shadows weave,
Whispers of truth that we believe.
Thoughts unspoken linger near,
In the stillness, we draw near.

With every breath, a sigh released,
In quiet realms, our souls find peace.
The language of the heart, profound,
In silence, all our hopes are found.

Remnants of What Was

In ruins lay the dreams once bold,
Stories woven, now silently told.
Ghosts of laughter, shadows of light,
Haunting the corners of the night.

Fragments glimmer in the gray,
Echoes of joy that fade away.
Time stands still, a patient friend,
In whispered winds, we comprehend.

What was lost, still whispers clear,
In every sigh, a trace is near.
Through heart's embrace, we hold the past,
In every moment, shadows cast.

In the Wake of Silence

In the wake of silence, futures bloom,
Softly weaving through the gloom.
A path unfolds, serene and wide,
Where dreams arise, and hopes abide.

Rippling gently like a stream,
Silence carries every dream.
In the hush, we start to see,
The beauty in tranquility.

Every heartbeat marks the time,
In silence, life begins to rhyme.
As echoes fade, we find our voice,
In quietude, we make our choice.

Torn Pages in a Worn Book

Faded ink tells stories lost,
Whispers of times dear, yet tossed.
Frayed edges catch the light,
Memories dance in the night.

Dusty corners hold the past,
Shadows of love that couldn't last.
Each crease a tale to unfold,
Life's tapestry, bittersweet, bold.

Leaves flutter like fragile hearts,
In the silence, the echo starts.
Names etched softly in the seam,
A book of dreams, a forgotten dream.

Once vibrant, now worn and pale,
Every chapter tells a tale.
Yet through the tears, hope still gleams,
In the margins, we find our dreams.

Torn pages speak of days gone by,
With every loss, new wings to fly.
Through the ragged, we still see,
The beauty of what used to be.

The Language of Broken Pieces

Shattered glass reflects the sky,
Silent echoes, a whispered cry.
Fragments of words hang in the air,
Unspoken thoughts linger, rare.

In the stillness, hearts collide,
Wounds exposed, no place to hide.
A tapestry of silence spun,
Connecting souls, yet overrun.

Missing fragments blur the truth,
Crumbling dreams of fading youth.
What once was whole, now torn apart,
Leaves quiet shadows on the heart.

Each broken piece tells a tale,
Of loves lost and dreams gone stale.
Amid the chaos, a spark ignites,
Resilience blooms in darkened nights.

Through fractured paths, we find our grace,
In shattered forms, we embrace.
The language of life speaks to us clear,
In broken pieces, love draws near.

An Unfinished Melody

Notes linger softly on the breeze,
A tune that dances through the trees.
Half-formed chords whisper and sigh,
Echoes of dreams that can't comply.

Each pause a breath, a chance to fill,
An empty space that longs to thrill.
The rhythm flows, then fades away,
Like fleeting hopes in disarray.

Fingers linger on the keys,
Searching for the flow that frees.
Unwrapped crescendos tease the soul,
Yet still, the silence takes its toll.

In the notes, a yearning glows,
For melodies that time bestows.
Yet in the gaps, new dreams arise,
An unfinished song beneath the skies.

A harmony of hope remains,
In every drop of joy and pain.
For life itself, a symphony,
In unfinished notes, we find the key.

Emptiness in Full Bloom

Petals fall from blossoms bright,
In beauty, they embrace the night.
An empty garden grieves the past,
Yet blooms still linger, unsurpassed.

Vibrant colors fade to gray,
Fields once rich now drift away.
Yet in the void, a quiet grace,
Offers solace in this space.

Sunshine warms the barren ground,
Life's resilience, a steady sound.
In emptiness, new roots take hold,
Unfolding stories yet untold.

Every stem stands brave and tall,
In emptiness, we rise from the fall.
From nothingness, hope finds its way,
In silent visions of the day.

So here we stand, in full bloom's reign,
Amidst the loss, we still find gain.
For in the heart of what we mourn,
Lies the promise of a new dawn.

The Weight of Uncarved Stone

In the quiet of the quarry,
Layers of time reveal their tale,
With each chisel's sharp embrace,
The heart of stone begins to pale.

Though rough edges fear the light,
They hold secrets deep within,
Unseen beauty waits in shadows,
To find freedom, it must begin.

Whispers of the artist's breath,
In every crack and crevice live,
Bound by the weight of silence,
Yet longing to forgive.

Time's gentle hand caresses fate,
As dust and dreams intertwine,
The uncut stone holds stories,
Of what's lost and what's divine.

Softly, the hammer strikes true,
Releasing power from beneath,
The weight of uncarved potential,
Shall find form in its own sheath.

Sifting Through Memories

In the attic of my mind,
Dust dances in golden rays,
Each box a timeworn passage,
Holding echoes of the days.

Faded photographs whisper,
Of laughter and love once shared,
Moments like grains of sand,
Through my fingers, they are bared.

Letters yellow with the years,
Ink has faded but not the heart,
Every word a thread of warmth,
Binding memories that won't depart.

Old toys lie in quiet corners,
Their stories long forgotten,
Yet beneath the layer of dust,
A child's joy remains unburdened.

As I sift through all that's lost,
I find pieces of my soul,
Rebuilding the tapestry of life,
To feel again, to feel whole.

The Silence After the Storm

In the wake of thunder's roar,
Stillness blankets all around,
Trees bow low, as if in prayer,
The world, a hushed, sacred ground.

Raindrops cling to leaves like tears,
Whispers of the tempest's song,
Nature breathes a heavy sigh,
A moment brief, yet feels so long.

Clouds disperse, revealing blue,
A promise masked in misty gray,
Like a heart that learns to heal,
Slowly finding its own way.

Footsteps soft on glistening earth,
Life begins to stretch and grow,
In the fragile, tender peace,
We find strength to bravely sow.

From the chaos, new roots thrive,
With each heartbeat, hope ignites,
In the silence after the storm,
We learn to cherish the lights.

Flickers of Hope Amidst Despair

In shadows deep, where dreams may falter,
A tiny spark still dares to glow,
Against the weight of heavy nights,
Flickers of hope begin to grow.

Each whisper of the fleeting light,
A testament to dreams held tight,
Though fears may rise like endless waves,
One flicker can ignite the fight.

Amidst the darkness, courage blooms,
A wildfire stoked by whispered prayers,
For even in the bleakest times,
A heart can find its way upstairs.

In every stumble, seeds are sown,
With each misstep, wisdom gains,
So hold the flickers close and warm,
In despair's grasp, our strength remains.

As dawn breaks through the shrouded night,
Those tiny flames will intertwine,
Filling the void with radiant light,
A dance of hope, eternally divine.

The Space Between Us

In shadows cast by silent night,
We linger far, yet hearts ignite.
A glance, a sigh, a tethered thread,
In every space, the words unsaid.

Across the void, a whisper grows,
Connecting souls, where love still flows.
With every beat, a bridge we weave,
In trust, we find what we believe.

The distance seems to fade away,
As dreams collide at the break of day.
In realms unseen, our spirits soar,
Together, always, forevermore.

In twilight's glow, the world retreats,
Yet in our hearts, the pulse still beats.
Through storms and calm, through night and dawn,
The space between will soon be gone.

So hold on tight, don't let it slip,
For love's a journey, not a trip.
In every heartbeat, there's a sign,
That you are yours, and I am mine.

Ripples in Still Water

A pebble dropped in quiet lake,
Creates a dance, the stillness wakes.
Each ripple spreads, a tale untold,
In water's embrace, the world unfolds.

The moonlight kisses surface clear,
A shimmer bright, so calm, so near.
With every wave, reflections gleam,
In silent depths, we chase a dream.

Time flows gently, an endless stream,
In tranquil moments, we find our theme.
Each heartbeat echoes, soft and low,
In stillness, wisdom starts to grow.

As nature breathes, we learn to trust,
In gentle sways, in honest rust.
For every drop of life we cast,
A ripple tells of futures past.

And when the storms begin to rise,
We seek the calm beneath the skies.
For in each tear, a chance we see,
Hope blooms again in harmony.

Ghosts of Yesterday

In corridors of faded light,
Echoes whisper of lost delight.
Each shadow passing, memories fade,
Yet in our hearts, they're never laid.

With every step, a story told,
Of dreams we chased, of hands we hold.
The past may haunt, but we stand tall,
In every rise, we heed the call.

Through time's embrace, we learn to grieve,
To find the strength in what we believe.
Ghosts linger on, but we move through,
In breaths of life, we start anew.

In haunted nights, we find our grace,
As time unveils a kinder face.
Each haunting whisper guides us near,
To futures bright, devoid of fear.

So cherish all the paths once crossed,
For even in loss, we're never lost.
In every tear, a lesson lies,
With every dawn, the spirit flies.

Learning to Breathe Again

In heavy silence, I pause and feel,
Unraveling dreams that time might steal.
With every breath, I seek the light,
To mend my soul, to take my flight.

The weight of sorrow drapes like night,
Yet hope ignites, a flicker bright.
With gentle steps, I learn to stand,
Embracing all, the soft and grand.

Each whispered prayer, a chance to grow,
Through valleys low, where wildflowers blow.
For every sigh, a promise made,
In heartbeats strong, the doubts will fade.

I gather strength from storms endured,
In moments lost, new visions stirred.
With every pulse, I find my way,
To brighter skies, to a brand new day.

So here I stand, with open heart,
In every breath, a work of art.
Learning slowly, piece by piece,
To breathe again, and find my peace.

The Beauty of Impermanence

Petals fall from the tree,
Whispers in the breeze,
Moments slip away,
Like shadows at dusk.

Time dances in cycles,
Each season a new song,
We embrace the change,
In all that feels wrong.

Fleeting are the colors,
In a sunset's last glow,
Life's impression is rich,
Yet soft like the snow.

A smile in the mirror,
Echoes of what once was,
Memories fade like fog,
But the heart still does pause.

From ashes a flower,
Grows fiercely with grace,
Find beauty in the dance,
Of time's warm embrace.

Tracing Footprints in the Sand

Waves kiss the shoreline,
An endless caress,
Footprints tell stories,
Of joy and distress.

With every step taken,
The tide washes clean,
Yet echoes remain,
Of where we have been.

Casting a glance back,
At journeys we've had,
Each mark holds a memory,
Of happy and sad.

Seagulls cry above,
As if to remind,
That fleeting the moment,
Yet loving is kind.

In twilight's soft glow,
New footprints appear,
As life keeps on moving,
With nothing to fear.

A Symphony of Goodbyes

In the fading light,
A soft farewell plays,
Each note lingers gently,
As time slips away.

Voices fade like echoes,
Lost in the embrace,
Every goodbye sung,
Leaves a tender trace.

A bittersweet chorus,
Of laughter and tears,
Memories compose
A song through the years.

As the curtain falls down,
We bow to the night,
In a world of goodbyes,
There's beauty in light.

And though we depart,
With heavy hearts sigh,
A symphony whispers,
We'll meet by and by.

When Love Shapes Grief

In the shadows of loss,
Love lingers so near,
A bittersweet echo,
Of what once was dear.

Holding onto the warmth,
Of memories past,
Each laugh and each tear,
In our hearts they are cast.

Time carves out our paths,
Through sorrow we tread,
Yet love is the thread,
That guides where we're led.

In whispers and sighs,
Their essence remains,
Through the depths of our grief,
Their spirit sustains.

So when love shapes our pain,
And shadows arise,
We carry their light,
While we learn how to rise.

The Sound of Lost Songs

Whispers dance in evening air,
Melodies of dreams laid bare.
Echoes fade, yet still they cling,
Notes of hope that silence brings.

Forgotten chords in twilight's hue,
Resonate with hearts so true.
Softly strummed on strings of fate,
A serenade we can't await.

In shadows cast by fading light,
The harmonies take flight tonight.
Each refrain, a breath of time,
Lost in rhythm, lost in rhyme.

Beneath the stars, a symphony,
Carried on a breeze set free.
For every song that drifts away,
New dreams await in night's ballet.

So let us sing what's yet to be,
In the echoes of memory.
The sound of lost songs lingers still,
Filling hearts with quiet thrill.

Seams of Solitude

In corners dark, the silence grows,
Where no one else but shadow goes.
Threads of life begin to fray,
In seams of solitude, they lay.

Whispers of a heart at rest,
Cradle dreams, yet feel no quest.
Stitching moments, one by one,
In quiet time 'til day is done.

Moments flicker, flame so slight,
Cloaked in stillness, shunned by light.
Raindrops tapping on the pane,
Echo solitude's soft refrain.

The fabric worn, but rich in thread,
In every tale that goes unsaid.
Seams of solitude will weave,
A tapestry that time won't leave.

Yet in this quiet, strength will rise,
From every tear, a new surprise.
A seamless dream, a heart's embrace,
In solitude, we find our place.

Portraits of Absence

In frames adorned with dust of years,
Lie portraits drawn from hidden tears.
Faces blurred, a haunting trace,
In the quiet, an empty space.

Time stands still in muted hues,
Memories fading, colors lose.
Each longing glance a crumpled sigh,
Whispered stories that drift and die.

Moments captured, forever lost,
In the gallery of all that's cost.
Echoes linger, shadows persist,
In the absence of the blissed.

Yet the heart knows the truth well,
In silence, we can hear them tell.
Portraits of absence, bittersweet,
Hold love's echo beneath our feet.

Through each frame, a light will gleam,
Remembered joys, a timeless dream.
And in that void, hope takes its stand,
For love transcends where time is banned.

The Journey Through Shadows

In the depths where darkness weaves,
A path emerges, heart believes.
Step by step, each choice we make,
Illuminates the dreams we chase.

Through twisted roads and whispered fears,
The journey pulls our truth from gears.
In every turn, a lesson learned,
From embers bright, new fires burned.

Beneath the cloak of night so deep,
Where secrets dwell and shadows creep.
Courage blooms in fragile light,
Guiding souls through endless night.

With every shadow, hope unveils,
A compass true when courage fails.
For through the dark, a dawn will rise,
Awakening the weary eyes.

So tread with care, but walk with grace,
In every shadow, find your place.
The journey through the night we roam,
Will lead the heart, forever home.

Mending the Torn Fabric

In shadows where threads unravel,
Hope whispers soft, a gentle travel.
Stitches bind the frayed edges near,
Creating warmth from threads of fear.

A needle glides, a patient hand,
Reforming dreams that once were grand.
Each knot a promise, woven tight,
Rebuilding dreams, igniting light.

With every tug, the fabric breathes,
Old wounds mend as the heart weaves.
Colors swirl in vibrant dance,
In every flaw, a second chance.

Time's embrace, a healing seam,
What was lost becomes the dream.
In laughter's thread and sorrow's weave,
We fashion joy, we learn to grieve.

The Softest Goodbyes

Beneath the stars, where shadows blend,
We shared our secrets, heart to mend.
Each word a feather, light and true,
Whispered gently, just me and you.

A touch, a sigh, our time unwinds,
In twilight's glow, the heart reminds.
Exhaling love, we part with grace,
Each goodbye leaves a warm trace.

Hands that linger, then drift apart,
Soft goodbyes echo in the heart.
In twilight's hush, we find our peace,
Releasing dreams, as sorrows cease.

With every step, memories bloom,
Filling the spaces, dispersing gloom.
In the quiet, hope still flows,
Softest goodbyes where kindness grows.

In the Garden of Memories

Amidst the blooms of fragrant past,
Memories linger, shadows cast.
Petals whisper of days gone by,
Underneath the vast, blue sky.

Steps on paths where laughter grew,
In each corner, a glimpse of you.
Sunlight dances on leaves so green,
Guarding truths that once were seen.

A tapestry of colors bright,
Every flower holds a light.
In this garden, hearts collide,
Growing stronger as they bide.

Among the thorns, soft tears may flow,
Yet in the pain, love starts to grow.
In every shade, a story waits,
Together, we embrace our fates.

Embracing the Void

In silent depths, where shadows dwell,
A quiet echo begins to swell.
The void calls out, both dark and deep,
Inviting thoughts that make us weep.

A canvas empty, vast and wide,
What will emerge when fears subside?
In solitude, I find my voice,
Learning to dance, unearth my choice.

Through the silence, I face the night,
Embracing dark to seek the light.
Each breath a promise, softly cast,
In every nothing, memories fast.

Yet in the void, hope takes its form,
Within the chaos, a quiet storm.
I gather strength, I learn to grow,
Embracing the void, I let love flow.

Beneath the Weight of Absence

In the silence, shadows stir,
Memories whisper, hearts defer.
Each echo lingers, yet feels far,
A distant light, a fading star.

Time ticks softly, moments fade,
A quilt of sorrow, threads displayed.
Longing wraps like winter's chill,
With every breath, a quiet thrill.

The clock may sway, the world turns fast,
Yet love remains, a haunting cast.
In spaces where you used to be,
Absence speaks, yet sets me free.

Each tear drops like a fragile stone,
Carving paths to the unknown.
Together once, now worlds apart,
Yet in my soul, you'll leave a mark.

Beneath the weight, I find my grace,
In shadows, I still see your face.
The tapestry of loss we weave,
In every thread, I still believe.

The Flavors of Nostalgia

Sweet like honey, moments blend,
A taste of time that will not end.
Lemon zest and salty waves,
Echoes of the life we crave.

Warm baked bread from an old kitchen,
The scent of love, my heart's condition.
Cinnamon whispers, stories unfold,
In each bite, a memory bold.

Summer evenings, laughter and cheer,
Fruity bliss, the sun so near.
Candied dreams in faded light,
Savoring all, a sweet delight.

Flavors mingle like friends at play,
Drawing us back to yesterday.
With every taste, a journey starts,
Nostalgia lives, in our hearts.

A banquet rich with life's embrace,
Through every morsel, time and space.
In the kitchen, love is stirred,
Each flavor shared, a magic word.

A Journey Through Unseen Roads

Dusty trails beneath my feet,
Uncharted paths, a tale to greet.
Each corner turned, a new delight,
In dawn's glow, adventure's light.

Mountains rise like giants strong,
Whispers of the earth's old song.
Through forests deep, shadows dance,
Nature calls, I take my chance.

Rivers weave a silver thread,
Guiding me where dreams are fed.
In silence found, I hear my name,
The wild beckons, spirits flame.

Stars above like lanterns bright,
Illuminating paths of night.
With every step, my soul expands,
Footprints etched in golden sands.

Unseen roads lead to the heart,
Adventures new, stories to chart.
In each detour, wisdom gleams,
Life unfolds in whispered dreams.

Resilience Amongst Ruins

Broken walls, a silent cry,
Yet in the cracks, the flowers vie.
Nature's gift, a life renewed,
From shattered hopes, a strength accrued.

With every storm, the heart grows bold,
Through ashes gray, a tale retold.
Fragments scattered, beauty's grace,
In rubble rests a warm embrace.

Time will weather, winds may howl,
Yet still we rise, our spirits prowl.
A phoenix born from dark despair,
With wings of courage, we repair.

Roots dig deep in ancient ground,
In scars we find a strength profound.
Amongst the ruins, life will dance,
Emerging strong, we take our stance.

Every crack, a story shared,
In resilience, we've always dared.
From shattered pasts, new dreams will bloom,
Amongst the ruins, we find room.

Shadows of Yesterday

In the twilight's gentle grasp,
Whispers linger, memories pass.
Ghosts of laughter, echoes near,
Shadows dance, they disappear.

Fading light on autumn's breeze,
Time has a way of bringing ease.
Footprints left on windswept ground,
In silence, past is still profound.

Veils of dusk, a solemn face,
Carried dreams in soft embrace.
Through the night, we softly roam,
Finding solace in the home.

Yet the morning's crimson glow,
Brings the truth, we come to know.
What was lost will find its way,
In hearts where shadows drift and sway.

So we cherish every thread,
Woven tales of things unsaid.
For in shadows, light can gleam,
Rekindling hope with every dream.

Heartstrings of Remembrance

Tangled notes, a haunting tune,
Whispered secrets with the moon.
Every moment, bittersweet,
Love that lingers, incomplete.

Threads of time exquisitely spun,
Binding stories of us as one.
In the silence, heartbeats call,
Echoes rise, then gently fall.

Pages turned, a faded book,
In the spine, my heart, it shook.
Every word, a breath of you,
In these lines, my feelings grew.

Time moves on, yet still I find,
Ghosts of you within my mind.
Heartstrings pulled, a tender ache,
In remembrance, love won't break.

So I hold on, though it pains,
To the heartstrings that remain.
For in each breath, a whisper stays,
Through the night, until the rays.

Fragments of Farewell

Underneath the autumn leaves,
Silent sighs and broken dreams.
In the distance, echoes play,
Fragments lost along the way.

Moments drift like falling snow,
Softly landing, then they go.
Each goodbye, a bitter taste,
Memories made, now laid to waste.

In a twilight, shadows creep,
Promises that we could not keep.
Words unspoken, left behind,
In the silence, futures blind.

Yet the stars begin to shine,
Carrying the weight of time.
For in fragments of our past,
Lessons learned, forever cast.

So we gather what remains,
Cherished joys and fleeting pains.
Through the heart, we learn to see,
Every farewell sets us free.

The Art of Letting Go

With a brush, I paint the night,
Colors fade, then take their flight.
In the canvas of my soul,
Lies the art that makes me whole.

Each stroke tells a story dear,
Of the moments I hold near.
Yet I learn to loosen ties,
In the quiet, courage lies.

Like the leaves that fall in grace,
Finding beauty in the space.
When I let go, I embrace,
Freedom found in empty place.

Trust the river's gentle flow,
Change will lead where hearts may go.
In surrender, strength can grow,
In the art of letting go.

So I cherish what has been,
While the new begins to spin.
With open arms, I'll rise and fly,
To the horizon, drawn to sky.

The Weight of Forgotten Smiles

In shadows where laughter used to play,
The echoes of joy now fade away.
A fleeting glance, a whispering trace,
Forgotten smiles in a lonely space.

Time weaves a tapestry of regret,
Moments lost, but we can't forget.
Each grin a story, a flickering flame,
Now just ashes, yet still bear a name.

Beneath the weight of all that we lack,
We seek the light, but there's no way back.
With every sigh, a piece of our heart,
Yearning for joy, yet drifting apart.

The heart remembers what the mind won't see,
Carrying shadows, forever set free.
Yet in each sorrow, a lesson is grown,
In the weight of smiles, we're never alone.

Remnants of Unspoken Words

In silence, secrets gather dust,
Words unsaid linger, a heavy rust.
A breath held tight, a story confined,
Echoing softly in the corridors of the mind.

They float like whispers on the breeze,
Longing for ears that seek to appease.
Promises made but left unvoiced,
Regrets that come with the choice of choice.

Each moment passed like grains of sand,
Slipping through fingers, we never planned.
In the chasm of thought, hope still resides,
Remnants of truths where the heart hides.

In the quiet, dreams often dwell,
Unraveled stories left to tell.
In the chamber of silence, we find our art,
Remnants of words that carry the heart.

Where Memories Linger

In corners where shadows tend to creep,
Memories flourish, awake from sleep.
Each photograph a story held tight,
Moments suspended, caught in soft light.

Fragrant echoes of laughter unfold,
Stories of past in colors bold.
We wander through halls lined with time,
Where joy and sorrow seamlessly climb.

The scent of old pages, worn and torn,
Whispers the tales of being reborn.
Faded letters and dreams longed for,
In the fabric of life, they forever soar.

When twilight paints the day's retreat,
We gather the past, bittersweet.
In the garden of thought, memories sing,
Where the heart finds home, and echoes take wing.

The Art of Letting Go

In the quiet dawn, a choice is made,
To release the burdens that once weighed.
Hands once clenched in a desperate grasp,
Now open wide, learning to unclasp.

With every tear, a weight lifts high,
Like the soft clouds drifting in the sky.
Embracing change, we start to breathe,
In the art of letting go, we believe.

The past, a canvas, we paint anew,
Colors of freedom, vibrant and true.
With each sunset, a promise to mend,
In the journey of letting go, a friend.

In the gentle whisper of the night,
We find our strength, we find our light.
With open hearts, we learn to forgive,
In the art of letting go, we live.

The Depths of Forgotten Laughter

In echoes dim, where shadows play,
A laughter lost, now fades away.
Forgotten tales beneath the skies,
Whispers of joy, in silent sighs.

Beneath the moon's soft, silvery glow,
Memories twirl, like leaves that blow.
Each chuckle haunted, sweet and deep,
In corners where old secrets sleep.

Once bright, the spark of joy now glum,
Yet in the heart, it starts to hum.
A fleeting joy, a fleeting chance,
In dreams, it still begins to dance.

Forgotten laughter, a distant chime,
Resonates through the threads of time.
Though faded now, a hint remains,
Of laughter lost, but joy untrained.

A Hearth of Memory

By the fire's glow, warmth does wane,
Stories rise like smoke and rain.
Each crackle brings a tale anew,
Of times long past, of me and you.

Embers flicker, shadows blend,
In this place, where hearts mend.
Memories dance in golden light,
A hearth of love, through day and night.

The flickering flames, they softly call,
Recalling faces, one and all.
Each moment shared, forever stays,
A timeless bond through endless days.

As darkness falls, the stars appear,
We gather close, our voices clear.
In warmth and laughter, life is sewn,
In this hearth, we feel at home.

Glimpses of What Remains

In faded photographs, we find,
The echoes lost, left far behind.
Fleeting glances, a soft embrace,
Glimpses of love in every trace.

Time's gentle hand, it blurs the view,
Yet memories linger, pure and true.
A tender smile, a whispered word,
In silent moments, voices stirred.

Through cracks of time, we peak and see,
The threads of life, they weave and free.
Lost faces haunt these silent halls,
In shadows cast, their spirit calls.

Though years may pass, and seasons change,
What remains feels so familiar, strange.
In every heartbeat, in every sigh,
Glimpses of love that never die.

Chasing Shadows of the Past

In twilight's glow, the shadows loom,
They whisper secrets from the gloom.
Chasing phantoms through the trees,
Where memories drift on the breeze.

Footsteps echo, soft and low,
Bearing tales of long ago.
In every crack, in every sound,
A piece of history is found.

The past entwined with present day,
In every laugh, in every sway.
Sketching stories on the walls,
As twilight fades, the night recalls.

Chasing shadows, we may stumble,
Yet in their dance, our hearts do humble.
For in the dark, we seek the light,
In every shadow, memories ignite.

Notes from a Wounded Heart

In shadows deep, the silence speaks,
A tender ache, a tear that leaks.
Memories swirl, both sweet and sore,
Each whispered thought, a heavy score.

Fragments swirl, like autumn leaves,
In gusts of wind, my spirit cleaves.
I write these lines, a silent cry,
For love once held, now passing by.

Beneath the stars, I seek my peace,
With every word, may sorrow cease.
The ink that flows, my solace brings,
In wounded hearts, the heart still sings.

Glimmers of Hope Amidst Grief

In the dark night, a candle glows,
A flickering flame, where courage grows.
Tears may fall, like rain from skies,
Yet through the pain, the spirit flies.

Soft whispers call, a gentle breeze,
Reminding souls that love can please.
Though loss may sting like winter's chill,
Hope's tender touch can heal and fill.

Each dawn arrives, a brand new start,
With morning light, it warms the heart.
In shadows cast, we find the way,
To cherish love, both night and day.

The Weight of Fond Farewells

Goodbyes linger like fading songs,
In empty halls, where memory throngs.
With heavy hearts, we wave and part,
Leaving behind a piece of heart.

Moments cherished, now framed in gold,
Stories shared, tenderly told.
With every hug, a silent pact,
In parting ways, we feel the act.

Yet in the ache, there's beauty found,
In bonds of love, we're truly bound.
Though distances grow, we hold them near,
In every farewell, love conquers fear.

Mirrors of Melancholy

Reflections cast in twilight's glow,
Haunted by dreams that ebb and flow.
Each glance reveals a tale untold,
In silver frames, the past unfolds.

Beneath the surface, a tempest brews,
As shadows dance, the heart must choose.
To seek the light, or dwell in pain,
In mirrors deep, we strive in vain.

Yet with each tear, a lesson learned,
In silent echoes, the heart has yearned.
To face the truth, to mend the soul,
In mirrors bright, we find our whole.

Unraveled Threads

In twilight's embrace, we weave our dreams,
Fingers touch the fabric of silent seams.
Each thread a story, a whisper of hope,
Frayed edges lingering, still learning to cope.

The loom of time spins with tender grace,
Beneath its rhythm, we find our place.
Colors blend where shadows have kissed,
Unraveled threads in a world of mist.

With every tug, the past comes undone,
Moments once lost, now dancing like sun.
In the tapestry of life, we find our way,
Each fiber a memory that will not sway.

Yet through the chaos, patterns emerge,
In jagged lines, our hearts converge.
Thread by thread, we gather the lost,
In this woven journey, we bear the cost.

So let us mend, through the tears we cried,
Reweave the fabric, with love as our guide.
In the tangled mess, beauty is found,
In unraveled threads, our souls unbound.

Remembering the Unseen

In whispers soft, the past does call,
Echoes of laughter, a comforting thrall.
Each moment cherished, though hidden from sight,
We gather the fragments, seeking the light.

The mirrors of time hold shadows so dear,
Reflecting the absence, we long to hear.
In the silence, the heart learns to yearn,
For stories once lived, for lessons discerned.

We wander through memories, lost in their maze,
Finding the joy in the bittersweet gaze.
In the tapestry woven of days gone by,
Unseen yet felt, like the stars in the sky.

With every heartbeat, their essence remains,
A dance in the breeze, through joys and the pains.
We honor the unseen each tear that we shed,
In remembering love, no words need be said.

So let us hold close, the warmth of the lost,
In the spaces between, we cherish the cost.
For those who have faded, in dreams they abide,
In the heart's quiet chamber, they never divide.

In the Echo of Their Laughter

In the echo of laughter, shadows play bright,
Moments suspended in soft, fleeting light.
Joy floats like petals upon summer air,
Each note a reminder of love, pure and rare.

Footsteps dance lightly on memories' ground,
In every heartbeat, their presence is found.
With each joyous sound, we rise and we fall,
In the echo of laughter, we answer the call.

Time weaves its magic, though faces may change,
In the music of laughter, nothing feels strange.
Bridges of smiles stretch across every space,
Connect us in ways that no time can erase.

Through valleys and mountains, the echoes resound,
Binding us closely, where joy can be found.
In every shared moment, our spirits take flight,
In the echo of laughter, hearts burn so bright.

So let us rejoice in the warmth that we share,
In the sweet serenade of love in the air.
For laughter's soft whispers will never grow dim,
In the echo of laughter, our souls dance on a whim.

Beyond the Horizon of Goodbye

Beyond the horizon, where dreams touch the sea,
A whisper of hope calls persistently.
With one last embrace, we let go of the past,
In the quiet farewell, love's shadows are cast.

Parting brings tears, yet also the gift,
Of memories treasured, where spirits uplift.
Each journey we're on leads down different roads,
In the bond of the heart, true connection unfolds.

Though distance may stretch, the stars still align,
In the vast emptiness, your essence is mine.
Through the silence of night, your voice, a sweet guide,
Beyond the horizon, you walk by my side.

Every sunset promises a rise anew,
In the cycle of life, where skies shift their hue.
So I carry your laughter, your light with me still,
Beyond the horizon, your love, a strong will.

Let hearts remain open to what lies ahead,
For in every ending, a new path is spread.
Beyond the horizon, where goodbyes may lie,
New beginnings awaken, as stars fill the sky.

Fragments of a Broken Heart

In the silence where shadows dwell,
Whispers of love begin to swell.
Shattered pieces on the floor,
Memories linger, begging for more.

Echoes of laughter, now just sighs,
Fading like stars in darkening skies.
Each fragment a tale, a once-shining dream,
Now lost in the cracks, or so it would seem.

Time stands witness to all that we feel,
Mending the wounds that time can heal.
Yet in this sorrow, a beauty resides,
In fragments of love, where hope abides.

Brittle and tender, a heart still beats,
Finding a rhythm in scattered retreats.
From ashes arise, as phoenix to flight,
Through brokenness flows a new kind of light.

In the end, the heart learns to sing,
Of healing and solace that moments can bring.
In shattered reflections, true strength we find,
In fragments of love, we are intertwined.

Healing Through the Cracks

From the depths of sorrow's night,
Emerges a flicker, a spark of light.
Through the cracks, new life will flow,
In hidden places, love will grow.

Soft whispers of kindness fill the air,
Woven together, a tapestry rare.
Each thread a story, a journey unique,
In healing through cracks, we find what we seek.

Time is a balm for wounds deep and wide,
As patience carries us like a tide.
With each passing wave, the heart starts to mend,
In the place of despair, new beginnings ascend.

Resilience blossoms in tender spaces,
Forged in the fire of fragile embraces.
Holding to hope, we release our fears,
In healing through cracks, we shed our tears.

The sun breaks through after clouds drift away,
Lighting the path for a brighter day.
With every heartbeat, our spirits renew,
Through cracks of the past, love shines ever true.

The Quiet After the Storm

When the tempest has passed, and the winds cease to howl,
Nature's breath deepens with a soft, soothing growl.
In stillness we gather the pieces once torn,
Finding solace in moments that follow the storm.

Birds begin to sing, the world feels anew,
Colors are vibrant, kissed by the dew.
Each leaf whispers stories of what came before,
The quiet after the chaos, a calming encore.

Clouds drift away, revealing the skies,
A canvas of dreams where hope now lies.
In silence we listen, the heart starts to learn,
That peace finds a way when the tides start to turn.

Gentle and soft, the light breaks through,
Illuminating shadows, as life starts to bloom.
With each passing moment, we breathe and align,
In the quiet after the storm, our hearts begin to shine.

Together we stand, hand in hand, side by side,
United in stillness, nowhere to hide.
In the echoes of thunder, a promise remains,
That peace follows heartache, as love breaks the chains.

When Time Stands Still

In a moment so fleeting, yet endless it feels,
A gaze that connects, a truth that reveals.
Time suspends breath in the hush of the night,
In silence we linger, wrapped in the light.

Every heartbeat resonates deep in our chest,
In the space between worlds, we find our true rest.
No future, no past, just the now we embrace,
When time stands still, we dwell in this place.

Lost in the magic that lingers and sways,
A dance of two souls in a delicate maze.
With whispers of dreams written in starlight,
When time stands still, everything feels right.

Captured in moments, as shadows descend,
The universe whispers, inviting our blend.
In the stillness, a promise, a bond to fulfill,
When time stands still, our hearts echo still.

Together we pause as the world falls away,
In the sanctuary of night, where dreams softly play.
A symphony of whispers, a tranquil thrill,
In the magic of now, when time stands still.

The Seasons of Grief

Winter whispers soft goodbyes,
Frozen tears beneath the skies.
Spring awakens with a sigh,
New blooms rise, and so must I.

Summer's warmth brings fleeting hope,
Memories drift like a tightrope.
Autumn leaves, they fall so slow,
In their dance, the heartache shows.

Each season marks a different path,
In shadows past, we learn to laugh.
The chill, the warmth, the colors blend,
In grief, we find we can amend.

Through every turn, our hearts do ache,
Yet through it all, new bonds we make.
Embracing loss, we learn to grow,
In seasons' change, we start to glow.

With every shift, the soul takes flight,
Grief's tapestry stitched with light.
We carry love through every phase,
In every tear, a spark ablaze.

A Canvas of Heartache

Brush strokes dark on a pale sheet,
A story told with each heartbeat.
Colors clash and slowly fade,
Yet beauty lives in love conveyed.

Scarlet reds and blues so deep,
Echoes of the pain we keep.
As layers build, the truth reveals,
In every stroke, the heart still heals.

Pale whites whisper of the past,
Memories held, like shadows cast.
Bright yellows bring a fleeting smile,
Through heartache, art can beguile.

Each tear becomes a vivid hue,
A canvas shaped by what we knew.
In everyday life's mundane fray,
Paint the heart and find the way.

As we blend and seek the light,
Our heartaches morph, take flight.
Through art, our pain finds voice,
In canvases, we gather choice.

Navigating the Wound

A compass whispers through the pain,
Each scar mapped out, a tale plain.
With every curve, a lesson learned,
Through stormy seas, the heart has turned.

Charting waters dark and vast,
Navigating shadows from the past.
In storms, we often lose our sight,
Yet hope still glimmers, bold and bright.

Lighthouses guard our fragile shores,
In search of peace, our spirit soars.
With every wave, we forge ahead,
In navigating grief, we're led.

The journey stirs both fear and grace,
Through every wound, we find our place.
An anchor holds as tides do change,
In healing hearts, we grow less strange.

With maps of love, we find our way,
Through troubled nights and dawning day.
In every wound, a story grows,
A testament to what we chose.

The Quiet Space of Reflection

In silence found, a room of peace,
Where echoes soften, thoughts release.
In quietude, the mind can roam,
A sanctuary, a cherished home.

Reflections dance upon the wall,
Each memory lingers in the thrall.
Whispers of what was once felt,
In this space, the heart can melt.

Beneath the weight of what we bear,
In gentle thought, we learn to care.
For in this stillness, insights gleam,
Guiding us softly toward our dream.

A candle flickers, shadows play,
Painting relief in soft array.
With every breath, the spirit sways,
In harmony with time's soft ways.

In gratitude, the heart reflects,
On all that's lost, yet each connects.
In quiet spaces, we embrace,
The beauty held in time and grace.

Sifting Through the Ashes

Among the embers, shadows creep,
Memories linger, secrets keep.
What once was bright, now fades to gray,
Hope lost in ashes, swept away.

In every spark, a tale resides,
Of laughter, joy, and reckless rides.
Yet in the ruins, we must find,
The strength to leave the past behind.

Cinders whisper of love's last breath,
Each fragment holds a scattered death.
We sift and sort, discerning grace,
In chaos, life finds its own place.

The air is thick with stories told,
Of valiant hearts and dreams of gold.
From dust we rise, reborn anew,
With every challenge, we push through.

So gather round the smoldering light,
Let it guide you through the night.
For even in ashes, embers glow,
Reminders of all we used to know.

A Palette of Pain

Brush strokes dance in hues of gray,
Each color speaks of loss and sway.
Crimson rivers bleed through the night,
In darkness, we search for the light.

Shadows flicker, whispers collide,
A symphony of hearts that cried.
Layers of sorrow, deep and vast,
Each moment cherished, never past.

Muted blues and vibrant greens,
Capture the dreams of what has been.
On this canvas, stories unveil,
Of shattered hopes that still prevail.

With every stroke, the heart weeps slow,
Yet still, the colors learn to grow.
In pain's embrace, we find our song,
A testament—the weak are strong.

So paint your hurt, let it be known,
For in each scar, a seed is sown.
A palette rich with shades of fate,
Turns bitter wounds to something great.

The Silence After the Clamor

When echoes fade, and stillness reigns,
The world withdraws its pounding pains.
In quiet corners, thoughts collide,
With every breath, what we can't hide.

The noise of life begins to wane,
As shadows stretch across the plain.
Listening close, we seek the truth,
In hushed tones, whispers of youth.

What once was chaos, fades to sighs,
In tranquil calm, the spirit flies.
The heart finds peace within the void,
Where clamor ceased, and dreams enjoyed.

A gentle stillness fills the air,
A moment found, a silent prayer.
In absence loud, we hear the beat,
Of life unfolding, bittersweet.

So let the silence wrap you tight,
Embrace the solitude of night.
For in this space, adornment lives,
The quiet gift that silence gives.

Surrendering to Remembrance

In twilight's glow, we pause and sigh,
Recalling moments, time gone by.
A tapestry of faces dear,
In memory's grasp, they still are near.

We gather time like precious stones,
Each shard of laughter, every groan.
In bittersweet, we find the grace,
Of love and loss in their embrace.

With every thought, a whisper calls,
Through gilded halls, our past enthralls.
We weave the threads, both joy and ache,
In shadows cast, our hearts awake.

And though the years like rivers flow,
In recollection, love will grow.
To surrender is to keep them close,
In every heartbeat, they are prose.

So let us hold what time won't claim,
In cherished moments, hearts aflame.
For every memory, sweet and bright,
Becomes a star that lights the night.

The Space You Left

In the quiet corners, shadows play,
Echoing laughter from yesterday.
Memories linger, soft and sweet,
In the emptiness, where we once would meet.

The chair sits vacant, untouched by time,
Your favorite book, a silent rhyme.
Each breath I take, whispers your name,
In the stillness, there's a gentle flame.

Sunlight falls softly on the floor,
Yet warmth it brings feels like a chore.
Every room tells a tale of you,
In every silence, the heart breaks anew.

Pictures hang, fragile and worn,
Reminders of love that'll never be torn.
I trace the moments, each grin, each tear,
In the space you left, I hold you near.

But even in sorrow, I find a way,
To honor the love, come what may.
For in this emptiness, I learn to grow,
The space you left, I now call home.

Navigating Grief's Labyrinth

In the maze of sorrow, I walk alone,
Each twist and turn, a heart turned to stone.
Memories echo in the darkened halls,
As I search for you, my spirit stalls.

Open doors lead to paths unseen,
Where shadows linger, quiet and keen.
I chase the whispers of what once was,
Trying to grasp the fleeting pause.

With every step, the weight it grows,
A heavy heart, where no one knows.
Yet in this journey, I seek a light,
To guide me through the endless night.

Time marks the walls with fading hues,
The scent of you in the morning dews.
Though the way is lost, I won't despair,
For love, it seems, is always there.

And as I wander through this plight,
I find my strength, it feels so right.
With each small step, I learn to cope,
In this labyrinth, I build my hope.

Beneath the Surface of Sadness

A river flows, deep and wide,
Hiding currents of pain inside.
Above the stillness, a calm disguise,
Yet below, the tumult never lies.

Each tear that falls, a drop in the stream,
Washing away what I thought was a dream.
Beneath the surface, emotions churn,
In the depths of quiet, I still yearn.

The sky may weep, yet I stay dry,
Masking the ache, the silent cry.
But deep down, where darkness thrives,
A flicker of hope reminds me I survive.

With every wave, I rise and fall,
Searching for strength, answering the call.
Adrift in shadows, I learn to swim,
Finding my way, even when it's grim.

For underneath sadness, life still flows,
In the depths of despair, resilience grows.
I seek the beauty that still remains,
Beneath the surface, a heart unchains.

The Colors of Mourning

Black and gray paint the world outside,
Each hue a reminder of love we can't hide.
In the palette of loss, shades intertwine,
A canvas of memories, soft and divine.

Chestnut browns of autumn leaves,
Whispering secrets of the heart that grieves.
The blues of twilight, calm yet forlorn,
As I navigate this path, so worn.

The crimson of sunsets reflects my ache,
A vivid reminder of all that's at stake.
Yet within the sorrow, gold threads shine,
A tapestry woven with love's design.

Each color tells stories, some bright, some dim,
Yet together they paint the life that had been.
In shadows and light, I find my way,
Through the colors of mourning, day by day.

And with every brushstroke, I honor you,
In the shades of my heart, the love still rings true.
For mourning is art, a journey we take,
In every color, a piece of you wakes.

The Unwritten Pages

In the silence of the night,
Dreams linger, taking flight.
Stories wait to be unfurled,
In the quiet of this world.

Blank pages whisper hope,
With every line, we learn to cope.
Fingers dance on empty space,
Yearning for the past to trace.

Thoughts like shadows, softly creep,
In the heart, secrets keep.
Words like colors wait to blend,
On blank pages, tales extend.

Tomorrow writes a brand new song,
In the ink of days gone long.
Each heartbeat, a step anew,
In the pages painted blue.

Voices echo, soft and clear,
As whispers fall on eager ear.
With every breath, a story wakes,
On unwritten paths, our heart breaks.

The Balance of Remembering

In the dance of joy and pain,
Memories flow like gentle rain.
With every heartbeat, shadows grow,
In the light, we learn to glow.

Past and present intertwine,
In the threads of time, they shine.
Holding close what slipped away,
In the echoes, we replay.

Faces fade, yet hearts remain,
Through laughter, through the strain.
Lessons etched in every tear,
The balance keeps us near.

Winds of change may sway our way,
Yet in the heart, the past will stay.
A tapestry of love and loss,
We wear our memories as a gloss.

Time will weave its ceaseless thread,
In the fabric of the dead.
As we walk this fragile line,
Remembering, we start to shine.

Ink from Tears

Every drop a story told,
Ink from tears, a heart of gold.
Writing pain on paper skies,
As the soul quietly cries.

Beneath the weight of sorrow's veil,
Words emerge, a haunting trail.
From the depths, emotions spill,
Inked reflections stand still.

Pages darkened, shadows cast,
Moments fade, yet memories last.
Each tear falls, a line to write,
In the darkness, we find light.

Filling pages with our plight,
Chasing shadows, seeking light.
Every word a bridge to peace,
From the pain, we find release.

With every stroke, healing starts,
Ink from tears becomes our arts.
Through the struggle, we find grace,
In our stories, we embrace.

Unfolding the Past

Like pages turning in the breeze,
The past whispers with such ease.
Memories dance in the fading light,
Guiding souls through day and night.

In the corners, shadows play,
Unraveled truths come out to stay.
Each moment captured, etched in time,
Unfolding the past, a silent rhyme.

Footsteps echo, soft and clear,
Lessons learned from those held dear.
With every glance, we start to see,
The threads that weave our history.

Time's embrace, a gentle hand,
Guiding us to sift through sand.
What was buried, now revealed,
In the past, our hearts are sealed.

As we turn, the past awakes,
In the choices that our heart makes.
Embracing stories, bold and vast,
In the journey of unfolding past.

The Gaps Between Us

In silence, shadows stretch and sway,
We linger in the words we say.
Distances carve our hearts in twain,
Yet hope remains to bridge the pain.

The spaces grow, a widening sea,
Where dreams collide and long to be.
With every heartbeat, close we tread,
On paths unseen, yet often led.

Yet in the gaps, a spark ignites,
A whispered breeze on starry nights.
Through unspoken fears we navigate,
And in the void, we find our fate.

Together still, though far apart,
The closeness dwells within the heart.
For every chasm, love will sway,
And fill the gaps in its own way.

The Fragility of Time

Moments dance on fleeting breath,
Each tick a reminder of life and death.
We grasp at sand that slips away,
In fragile threads, we weave our play.

The ticking clock, a gentle guide,
Through rivers of time, we drift and slide.
Past whispers call, yet futures shine,
In every heartbeat, fate aligns.

Today may fade, tomorrow's dawn,
As shadows stretch on virtue drawn.
In fragile hours, we build and break,
Treasures forged for memory's sake.

The threads of time entwine our souls,
In every story, truth unfolds.
Hold tight the twine that binds us fast,
For fleeting seconds seldom last.

Unraveling Threads

In tangled yarns of fate we find,
A tapestry of heart and mind.
With every pull, a story spools,
As life unwinds, our spirit schools.

Each thread connects, though frays may meet,
In colors bright, our joys repeat.
Twists and turns, we dance with fate,
Unraveling threads, we cultivate.

Through frayed edges and knots that bind,
We treasure what we leave behind.
A woven tale, a patchwork bright,
Unraveled, yet we find our light.

Embrace the mess, the beauty raw,
In countless threads, we see the flaw.
For every tear, a lesson learned,
In unraveling, our hearts are turned.

Embracing the Echo

In whispered winds, the echoes play,
A melody of yesterday.
With every sound, the past ignites,
As shadows of old fill moonlit nights.

Embrace the echoes, soft and clear,
In every note, a memory dear.
The haunting calls, the laughter shared,
In echoes long, our hearts are bared.

Through laughter's rise and sorrow's fall,
The echoes linger, heed their call.
They guide us home through paths of light,
And keep our spirits ever bright.

In every pause, a moment glows,
Where echoes deep within us grow.
In harmony, we find our way,
Embracing echoes every day.

In the Wake of Heartache

Whispers carried on the breeze,
Memories weave through rustling trees.
A shadow falls where laughter played,
In echoes soft, the heart is swayed.

Grief dances lightly on my skin,
Each step a reminder of where I've been.
Yet in this ache, I find my grace,
Resilience blooms in a desolate space.

The sun dips low, the sky turns red,
With every tear that I have shed.
Moonlight kisses the scars I bear,
A gentle touch, a tender care.

In the quiet, I hear the call,
Of love that lingers, though shadows fall.
With time, the heart begins to mend,
And learns to dance, my steadfast friend.

So here I stand, both strong and free,
In the wake of all that's left of me.
Through heartache's storm, I'll choose to rise,
For in the dark, the spirit flies.

Navigating Empty Rooms

Footsteps echo on barren floors,
Open windows and silent doors.
Each room a chapter, tales untold,
In shadowed corners, memories hold.

I walk through spaces once alive,
Where laughter lingered, hopes would thrive.
But time has turned the key, it seems,
And left me wandering through lost dreams.

Dust motes dance in fading light,
A ghostly waltz of day and night.
The walls still whisper, yet I roam,
These empty rooms, they feel like home.

I collect the echoes like old friends,
In every silence, a story bends.
Though they're hollow, they hold my heart,
A tapestry where I won't part.

I find the beauty in what's gone,
In quiet moments, I move on.
Navigating through the dim and vast,
I hold the present, and learn from the past.

The Color of Sorrow

Sorrow paints in shades of grey,
A canvas stretched where shadows play.
Each stroke a tear, each line a loss,
In every corner, a heavy gloss.

Yet within this palette, colors blend,
A symphony that time will send.
For every dark, there's light to find,
In sorrow's grip, we're intertwined.

Through hues so deep, I learn to see,
The strength that blooms, the heart's decree.
With each brushstroke, pain takes flight,
Transforming loss into pure light.

The moments spent in quiet grief,
Are brushstrokes wise, the mind's belief.
In sorrow's shade, we cradle dreams,
And find the beauty in tender seams.

So let it rain, let colors flow,
For in the dark, our spirits grow.
The canvas waits, our story sings,
In the color of sorrow, hope takes wings.

Finding Light in the Dark

When shadows fall and silence creeps,
Hope flickers soft, in stillness, we keep.
A spark ignites within the cold,
A flame that flickers, brave and bold.

I search for whispers in the night,
For stars that shimmer, piercing light.
Each breath a promise, each heartbeat true,
In the dark, we find what's due.

Through tangled thoughts and heavy fears,
I journey on, embracing tears.
For even in the deepest void,
Our spirits rise, unbroken, buoyed.

With every dawn, a chance to heal,
The sun's warm touch, a gentle feel.
Finding light where shadows roam,
In darkness, we carve out our home.

So here I stand, with open heart,
In search of light, I play my part.
For in the dark, I've come to see,
The brilliance that resides in me.

Beneath the Weight of Loss

In shadows deep, a heart does ache,
Memories linger, each breath we take.
Phantoms whisper, voices soft and clear,
We carry burdens, year upon year.

Time moves on, yet still we stand,
A fragile thread, a trembling hand.
Chasing echoes, lost in the night,
We grasp at fragments, seeking the light.

Within the silence, tears start to flow,
The weight of loss, a heavy blow.
In quiet moments, love remains,
A bittersweet song, a heart that pains.

Hope flickers dim, but never fades,
In every shadow, a light cascades.
Beneath the weight, we learn to grow,
From seeds of sorrow, new roots will show.

Tomorrow's Promise in Today's Grief

Today we mourn, in shadows we hide,
Yet tomorrow's promise walks by our side.
In every tear, a story untold,
A whisper of hope, both gentle and bold.

The dawn may break with colors anew,
Yet here in the silence, grief holds us true.
Each heartbeat echoes the life we once knew,
In the depths of sorrow, love still shines through.

Together we gather, with hands intertwined,
In shared understanding, solace we find.
Though paths may diverge, we honor the past,
In memories cherished, our bonds hold fast.

Tomorrow will come, with skies painted bright,
Yet today we treasure the stars of the night.
In every goodbye, tomorrow's embrace,
A cycle of life, a sacred space.

Echoes of Absence

The room is quiet, whispers remain,
Echoes of laughter, entwined with the pain.
Each corner holds fragments, moments in time,
In silence we search for rhythm and rhyme.

Absence lingers, a heavy shroud,
Yet love's sweet promise still speaks loud.
Fading footsteps, yet vivid in mind,
A tapestry woven, tenderly designed.

In the heart's chamber, memories dwell,
Tales of joy woven in a spell.
What once was light, now shadows cast,
Yet within those echoes, a love that lasts.

In solitude, a song begins to rise,
A melody sweet, despite goodbyes.
Through echoes of absence, we learn to see,
The beauty of love, eternally free.

The Weight of Unsaid Goodbyes

Words left unspoken, heavy as stone,
A chasm between us, we walk alone.
In the quiet, our thoughts collide,
Yet the weight of silence, we cannot hide.

Each glance tells stories we dare not say,
Unsaid goodbyes, they linger and stay.
In the depth of longing, hearts intertwine,
Yet fear holds us back, a shadowy sign.

A breath catches softly, a tear's slow fall,
In the weight of unexpressed, we feel it all.
The beauty of moments, lost in the fray,
When the heart yearns for words that drift away.

Time may soften the edges of pain,
Yet memories echo in joy and disdain.
We carry the burdens, both heavy and light,
In the weight of goodbyes, we seek the light.

Where Teardrops Fall

In quiet rooms where shadows sigh,
A drop descends, a heavy cry.
Memories linger, soft and small,
Each one echoes where teardrops fall.

Time drips slowly, stained with grief,
In every frame, the loss feels brief.
Yet in the silence, love stands tall,
Forever near where teardrops fall.

Faces fade, but their warmth stays,
In whispered winds and golden rays.
Through the sorrow, they enthrall,
As spirits dance where teardrops fall.

Hope finds ways to touch and heal,
Even when wounds seem too real.
In every heart, a gentle call,
Resilience blooms where teardrops fall.

So let each tear be like a stream,
Flowing softly, a sacred dream.
In every heart, we answer all,
Together we rise where teardrops fall.

Threads of Time

In the tapestry of days gone by,
Threads weave stories, low and high.
Softly pulling memories fine,
Stitched together, threads of time.

Every moment a stitch so bright,
Woven gently, day and night.
As the fabric dances, we align,
Holding close these threads of time.

Time unravels, yet it's a gift,
A playful breeze that helps us lift.
In silver linings, we define,
Our essence held in threads of time.

Love and laughter, pain and cheer,
We gather close, those we hold dear.
With every heartbeat, we entwine,
Embracing life, these threads of time.

Through every storm and sunny climb,
Each moment cherished, so sublime.
From past to future, we align,
Crafting hope in threads of time.

Embraces Without Arms

In a crowded room, yet feeling alone,
Hearts connect in the silence grown.
Without the touch, we still disarm,
Finding strength in embraces without arms.

Words unspoken, a shared glance,
In fleeting moments, we find our dance.
Together in spirit, we stay warm,
Wrapped in love's embrace without arms.

Time may distance, yet bonds remain,
In all the joy and the bittersweet pain.
We hold each other, safe from harm,
In the quiet of embraces without arms.

Memories linger, a soft refrain,
A gentle presence that soothes the pain.
In every heartbeat, we feel the charm,
Finding solace in embraces without arms.

So when the world feels out of reach,
Look within, for love will teach.
In every moment, we find a balm,
In the depths of embraces without arms.

Surviving the Aftermath

After the storm, in shadows cast,
We gather strength from days long past.
Through wreckage, we learn to stand,
    Finding hope in the aftermath.

Life now unfolds in pieces strewn,
With every dawn, we greet the new.
From ashes rise, like trees so grand,
    Rebirth sings in the aftermath.

Whispers of resilience fill the air,
In every heart, we learn to care.
Together, we venture hand in hand,
    Finding courage in the aftermath.

Tears may fall, but we will rise,
Building dreams under wide-open skies.
To reclaim joy, our spirits expand,
    Embracing life in the aftermath.

Through trials faced, we find our way,
Each step forward, a brighter day.
In every heartbeat, love's command,
    We flourish still in the aftermath.

The Heart's Silent Cry

In the stillness, whispers fade,
A longing heart, quietly betrayed.
Soft shadows dance upon the wall,
Echoes of love, a silent call.

Tears that fall, like rain from skies,
Yet no one hears the heart's soft sighs.
Beneath the surface, pain resides,
A hidden world where sorrow hides.

Hope flickers dim, like a candle's light,
Guided by dreams that take to flight.
In every beat, a story lies,
The heart's own song, it softly cries.

Gentle moments spin like thread,
In the tapestry of words unsaid.
Fingers trace what once was there,
A haunting melody fills the air.

Yet in the silence, love remains,
Life's cruel dance, a storm of gains.
With every breath, the heart complies,
Forever bound to its silent cries.

Traces of What Wasn't

Footprints linger on the sand,
Memories drift, like grains unplanned.
In twilight's glow, shadows remain,
A whisper lost in fleeting strain.

Fragile moments, threads undone,
What could have been, now just a pun.
Dreams once painted in vibrant hue,
Now fade to gray, a careful view.

The echoes ring of choices missed,
Like fleeting dew, lost in the mist.
In every smile, a hint of pain,
Traces of joy, now bittersweet rain.

Paths not taken, roads ignored,
In the heart's map, silence stored.
Each step away, a haunting trace,
Of what was lost, no time or space.

With every sunset, shadows grow,
Reflecting dreams we didn't sow.
Yet life moves on, though we might pine,
For traces of what wasn't, divine.

Echoes of Laughter in the Silence

In quiet corners, laughter hides,
Like fleeting joy that gently glides.
In empty rooms, where shadows play,
Memories dance, though words decay.

Laughter lingers on the breeze,
A ghostly tune that seeks to please.
In silence deep, a melody grows,
Echoed smiles, like painted rose.

Soft whispers carry tales of cheer,
A symphony that draws us near.
Through the hush, the heart can feel,
A warmth in moments, so surreal.

Yet silence stretches, stark and wide,
Where echoes of laughter once did bide.
In the quiet, we find a way,
To cherish joy that went astray.

So let us weave, with threads of light,
Our laughter back into the night.
For in the dark, the heart can find,
The echoes of love, forever blind.

The Curtain of Memory

Behind the curtain, shadows creep,
Each glimpse a promise, buried deep.
Fading pictures, moments caught,
Whispers linger in every thought.

Curtains raise, revealing time,
A bittersweet dance, a silent rhyme.
With each recollection, a story starts,
Tied by the threads of longing hearts.

Pages turn, the past unfolds,
In the quiet, destiny holds.
Each layer peeled, another chance,
Awakens memories to dance.

Yet time is fickle, swiftly flows,
What once was bright, now seldom glows.
The curtain falls, the stage is bare,
In the silence, we learn to care.

For every scene, a lesson learned,
A flicker of hope, in hearts that yearn.
Behind the curtain, life goes on,
In the remnants where dreams are drawn.

Whispers of Absence

In the corners of my mind,
Your laughter softly fades,
A gentle echo lingered,
In the silence, memories wade.

Empty chairs at evening dusk,
Hold the shadows of your smile,
A presence felt yet out of reach,
Time's cruel trick, yet I stay awhile.

Winds carry whispers, bittersweet,
As if you were still near,
In every rustle of the leaves,
Your spirit's touch I hear.

Photographs with edges worn,
Capture moments, frozen light,
But behind the smiles a void,
Where your essence once took flight.

Night brings dreams of tender grace,
A dance beneath the stars,
Though you've slipped beyond my grasp,
Your love forever scars.

Echoes in Silence

Beneath the moon's silver glow,
Silence whispers your sweet name,
Each breath a reminder of
The spark that once brightly claimed.

Footsteps fade on twilight paths,
Where laughter filled the air,
Now shadows stretch long and lean,
In the stillness, I lay bare.

Moments freeze in empty rooms,
Walls hold stories left untold,
Echoes of our shared heartbeat,
In memories that won't grow old.

Stars blink in sorrow's embrace,
As I navigate the dark,
Trying to find the path again,
In quiet, I search for the spark.

Time drips slow, a heavy weight,
Yet hope flickers gently still,
In the silence, voices linger,
A testament to love's strong will.

Shadows of What Was

In the corners of faded dreams,
Your silhouette does dwell,
Casting shadows on bright days,
Where joy once chose to swell.

Each memory a bittersweet taste,
Like wine turned sour with age,
What was vibrant now lies bare,
As we turn a fragile page.

The laughter we shared haunts the halls,
As silence fills the space,
I chase phantoms in the air,
Desiring your warm embrace.

Days bleed into night's cold arms,
While time slips through my grasp,
Yet under layers of grief's shroud,
Your spirit I still clasp.

Radiance dims with every dawn,
Yet some glimmers still remain,
A reminder of our bond,
In the shadows of my pain.

A Journey Through Grief

With every step, I tread so slow,
A path lined with whispered sighs,
Grief packs its heavy baggage,
As I navigate the lies.

Each day a mountain to be climbed,
The summit out of sight,
Yet I carry you within my heart,
Your love, my guiding light.

Raindrops fall, a soft lament,
For moments lost in time,
Yet through the tears a spark ignites,
A resilience born from rhyme.

Seasons change, the world spins on,
While I stand still in thought,
Memories like autumn leaves,
In every gust, I'm caught.

Yet in this journey through the dark,
A dawn will break anew,
For love's a path that never ends,
And leads me back to you.

The Tides of Remembrance

In the ebb and flow of time,
Memories wash on the shore,
Each wave a whisper of days,
That linger forevermore.

Shells hold secrets of the past,
In the sands, stories unfold,
The tides bring gifts of yesterday,
As future dreams are told.

Underneath a setting sun,
Reflections dance on the crest,
Carried off by the ocean,
Where heart and soul find rest.

Time's currents pull and sway,
Yet some things never wane,
Love remains a constant tide,
That eases every pain.

As night descends and stars align,
The moonlight guides the way,
In every swell, a heartbeat,
That speaks what words can't say.

A Dance with the Unfamiliar

In moonlit fields of shadows,
The unknown calls to me,
A waltz upon the twilight,
Where spirits roam so free.

Each step I take is cautious,
Yet joy ignites my heart,
With every twist and turn,
I weave my brand new start.

The wind it sings a soft tune,
As whispers fill the air,
A dance of vibrant colors,
A tapestry so rare.

Faces of the past emerge,
Their laughter fills the night,
In this embrace of shadows,
I lose myself in light.

With every beat, I'm growing,
In the rhythm, I belong,
A journey into mystery,
Where I become the song.

Shadows on the Wall

In a dim-lit room of silence,
Shadows flicker, sway, and dance,
Echoes of forgotten dreams,
In the stillness, they entrance.

Figures stretch and twist in twilight,
Each move tells a tale unspun,
A theatre of the lonely,
Where broken hearts come undone.

Faint whispers linger softly,
In the corners of my mind,
A reminder of the moments,
Left in darkness far behind.

Yet from these shadows, light can break,
A flicker of hope, a spark,
In the depths of shadow's clutch,
A chance to mend the dark.

So I watch the play unfolding,
With lessons written on the wall,
In shadows deep, the truth may lie,
I rise, I stumble, I crawl.

In the Depths of Reflection

Beneath the surface of still waters,
I dive into the depths so clear,
Where echoes of my thoughts emerge,
And every fear I hold draws near.

Ripples ripple through my mind,
Companions to the silent ache,
In the depth, I seek the truth,
In shadows, I bend and break.

The mirror of the soul reflects,
With images both bright and dim,
Each glance unveils a layer deep,
Inviting me to swim.

Thoughts ascend like bubbles rise,
Carrying whispers from the past,
In the quiet of reflection,
I learn to breathe at last.

Underwater, I find solace,
In every wave of gentle grace,
For in the depths of self-discovery,
I finally find my place.

Seeds of Remembrance

In quiet earth, the seeds are sown,
Whispers of stories, softly grown.
Each memory sprouts, a vibrant leaf,
Nurtured by love, despite the grief.

Time weaves through roots, deep and wide,
Binding the past with the present's tide.
In every bloom, a face appears,
Bringing forth laughter, watering tears.

Under the sun, they dance and sway,
Echoes of voices, never far away.
With gentle hands, we tend the ground,
In every heartbeat, their light is found.

Seasons change, yet they remain,
Symbols of joy, and of pain.
A garden of hope, where shadows fall,
Seeds of remembrance blossom for all.

Through the storms, they rise and thrive,
Carrying whispers of those alive.
Each petal tells of love once known,
In this sacred space, I'm never alone.

Dust and Echoes

In abandoned halls, dust dances light,
Echoes of laughter fade into night.
Walls hold stories of moments spent,
Lingering whispers, a life well bent.

Footsteps tread on the wooden floor,
Every creak reveals an unseen door.
Ghosts of the past in shadows roam,
Longing for warmth, a fragile home.

Time stretches thin, like a delicate thread,
Connecting the living and those long dead.
In stillness, their presence we can feel,
A tapestry woven, both fragile and real.

Sunbeams filter through the cracks,
Painting memories in silver's tracks.
With every sigh, the age-old sighs,
Tell of the dreams that never die.

Through dust and echoes, life persists,
In the silence, a quiet twist.
We gather the moments, old and dear,
In every corner, ghosts draw near.

Threads of Lost Time

In the loom of life, threads intertwine,
Moments of joy and sorrow align.
Each strand a story, vivid and bright,
Fading in shadows, lost to the night.

Woven in silence, the tapestry waits,
Holding the weight of forgotten fates.
In every knot, a memory clings,
A vivid reminder of fleeting things.

Time slips through fingers like grains of sand,
Precious and fragile, it slips from our hand.
Yet in the fabric, the past remains,
Stitched to our hearts with invisible chains.

As we unravel what once was near,
We find the laughter, we find the tears.
Each thread tells tales of love and strife,
Binding us still, in the saga of life.

Though threads may fray, they never break,
In the quilt of existence, our stories awake.
We cherish the patchwork with each new dawn,
For in the lost time, we keep moving on.

Reflections in a Shattered Mirror

A broken mirror reflects our fears,
Shards of memories, laughter and tears.
In every fragment, a piece of truth,
Tangled in time, the wisdom of youth.

The edges sharp, they catch the light,
Revealing glimpses of love and plight.
In twisted images, we search for grace,
Finding our essence in a fractured space.

Each shard a story, a moment's glance,
The beauty in chaos, a fleeting chance.
Though jagged lines divide and sway,
Together they tell of a brighter way.

Through shattered glass, we see anew,
The hidden parts that once we knew.
Reflections shimmer, in colors bright,
Guiding lost souls back into the light.

Embrace the pieces; they make us whole,
Fragments of life, the heart's console.
In the mirror's depths, we find our way,
Reflections of love that never fray.

Carved in Memory

In whispers soft, the shadows dance,
Echoing tales of fleeting glance.
A time once shared, etched deep inside,
Moments cherished, where love would bide.

Faded photographs, stories unfold,
Fragments of laughter, memories bold.
Each heartbeat lingering, a gentle sigh,
In the quiet night, our love draws nigh.

Little reminders, a scent in the air,
A smile, a touch, as if you were there.
With every shadow, I trace your name,
In the realm of dreams, we'll never be tame.

Yet time flows on, a river so wide,
With currents of change, we must abide.
Though apart in distance, together in heart,
Carved in memory, we'll never depart.

When twilight falls and stars ignite,
I hold your spirit, burning bright.
In the fabric of time, we'll find our place,
Forever woven, in love's embrace.

Tides of Sorrow

Waves crash hard upon the shore,
Whispers of loss that grip and implore.
Each tide a reminder of time gone by,
In the depths of sorrow, I learn to sigh.

The moon weeps light into the night,
Guiding the hearts that fight the fright.
Each ebb and flow a dance of pain,
Yet in the struggle, love will remain.

Raindrops fall like tears from the sky,
As memories linger, too hard to deny.
But as the sea retreats from the land,
Hope rises slowly, offered by hand.

With every heartbeat, grief may fade,
Through shadows cast, new dreams are laid.
Sorrow's tide, though heavy and long,
Will shape my heart, making me strong.

In the quiet dawn, I will rise anew,
Finding the strength that carries me through.
For in the sorrow, there lies a spark,
Guiding me gently, from light into dark.

The Anatomy of Heartbreak

Pieces scattered, like autumn leaves,
A heart laid open, as the silence grieves.
Each fragment a memory, sharp as a knife,
In the gallery of loss, I search for life.

Veins of longing pulse deep in the night,
Echoes of laughter, visions of light.
But shadows linger, whispering tales,
Of promises broken, of love that pales.

Blueprints of dreams now faded and torn,
In the anatomy of heartbreak, I'm reborn.
From ashes of longing, new love may rise,
As the heart learns to heal, and pain slowly dies.

Though scars may remain, a testament true,
To the battles fought, and the love that was due.
With each tender beat, resilience awakes,
Crafting a vessel that time softly makes.

In the depths of the night, I will find my way,
Tracing the lines where my heart used to sway.
For in every ending, there lies a start,
The anatomy of heartbreak, a map of the heart.

Finding Light in the Dark

In shadows deep, where echoes dwell,
Hope flickers faintly, casting its spell.
The heart may tremble, the mind may doubt,
But a spark ignites, a whisper, "Hold out."

Through the thorns of despair, I gently tread,
Each step a promise, a path I've shed.
With every sunrise, a canvas of gold,
The beauty of struggle, the story unfolds.

Stars wink kindly from heavens afar,
Guiding the lost, like a shining star.
In the quiet moments, I breathe and believe,
That light from within is the gift I receive.

Lessons learned in the depths of my soul,
Finding the pieces that make me whole.
In the tapestry woven with threads of gray,
I discover my strength in this vibrant display.

So here in the dark, I stand tall and proud,
Embracing the light that breaks through the cloud.
For in every shadow, there's brilliance to find,
A beacon of hope, forever entwined.

Milton Keynes UK
Ingram Content Group UK Ltd.
UKHW021629011224
451755UK00010B/537